# Think Before You Act

Think before you act.

**Eat healthy foods so you'll grow.**

Mind your parents, oh, oh, oh.

Every day, you need self-control.

5

Having self-control will help you
meet your goals, oh, oh, oh.

Keep your hands to yourself.

Just say "no."

Walk away from a fight, oh, oh, oh.

Every day, you need self-control.

10

Having self-control will help you meet your goals, oh, oh, oh.

11

Finish your work.

Be careful where you go.

Spend your money wisely, oh, oh, oh.

Every day, you need self-control.

Having self-control will help you
meet your goals, oh, oh, oh.